Theory Paper Grade 4 2010 A
Model Answers

OPY

1 (a) tenderly / affectionately (2)
accent / forced / accented (1)

(b)  / 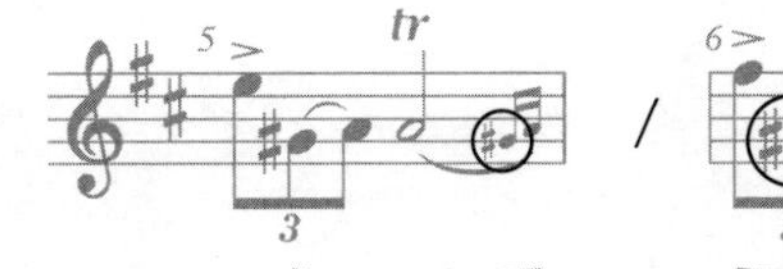 / 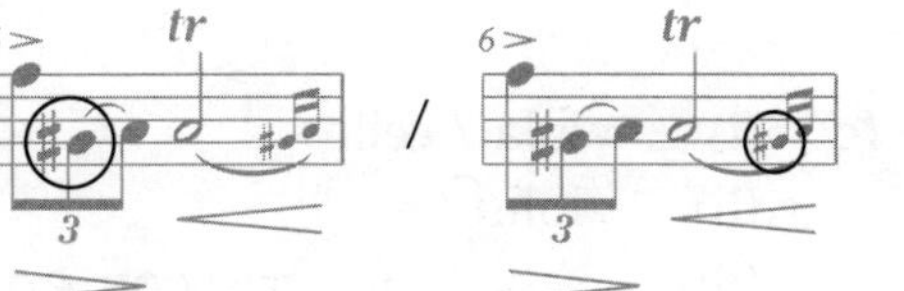 (2)

(c) grace notes (2)

(d)  (3)

(e) 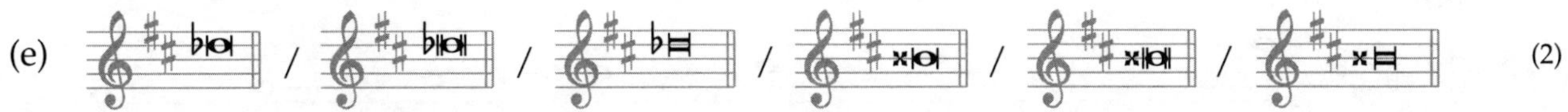 (2)

(f) (3)

2 *There are many ways of completing this question. Either of the specimen completions below would receive full marks.* (10)

EITHER

(a)

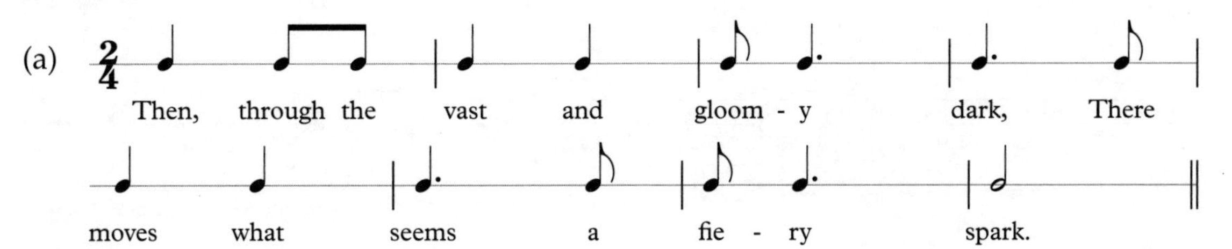

OR

(b)

3 (a) (i) comfortably / conveniently (2)
in a singing style (2)
simple / plain (2)

(ii) (4)

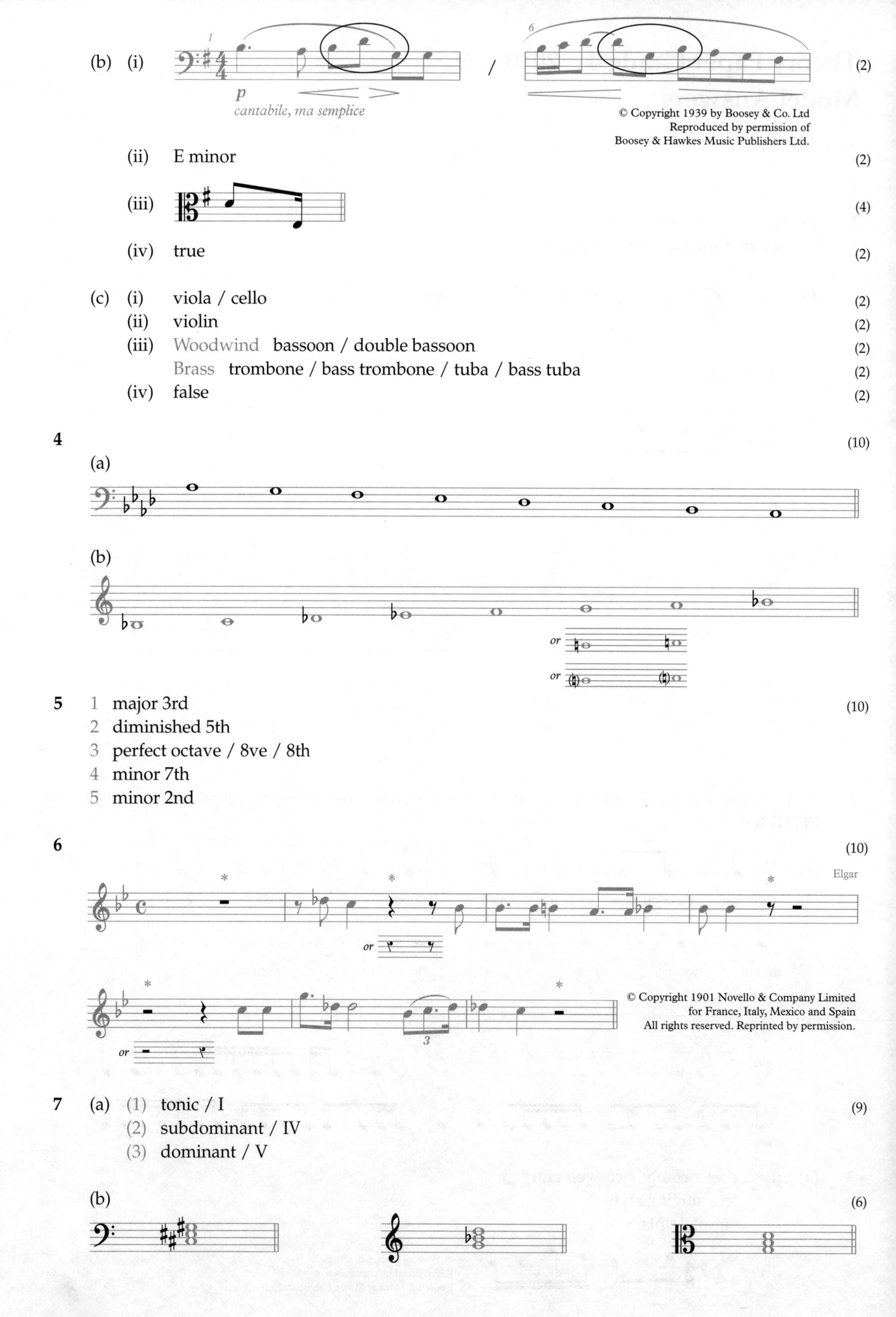
(b) (i)
p
cantabile, ma semplice
(2)
© Copyright 1939 by Boosey & Co. Ltd
Reproduced by permission of
Boosey & Hawkes Music Publishers Ltd.
(ii) E minor (2)
(iii) (4)
(iv) true (2)
(c) (i) viola / cello (2)
(ii) violin (2)
(iii) Woodwind bassoon / double bassoon (2)
Brass trombone / bass trombone / tuba / bass tuba (2)
(iv) false (2)
4 (10)
(a)
(b)
or
or
5 1 major 3rd (10)
2 diminished 5th
3 perfect octave / 8ve / 8th
4 minor 7th
5 minor 2nd
6 (10)
Elgar
or
or
© Copyright 1901 Novello & Company Limited
for France, Italy, Mexico and Spain
All rights reserved. Reprinted by permission.
7 (a) (1) tonic / I (9)
(2) subdominant / IV
(3) dominant / V
(b) (6)
4

Theory of Music Exams

MODEL ANSWERS

GRADE 4

2010

Welcome to ABRSM's *Theory of Music Exams Model Answers*, Grade 4, 2010. These answers are a useful resource for pupils and teachers preparing for ABRSM theory exams and should be used alongside the relevant published theory exam papers.

All the answers in this booklet would receive full marks but not all possible answers have been included for practicable reasons. In these cases other reasonable alternatives may also be awarded full marks. For composition-style questions (where candidates must complete a rhythm, compose a melody based on a given opening or set text to music) only one example of the many possible answers is given.

For more information on how theory papers are marked and some general advice on taking theory exams, please refer to the booklet *These Music Exams* by Clara Taylor, which is available free of charge and can be downloaded from www.abrsm.org.

Using these answers

- Answers are given in the same order and, where possible, in the same layout as in the exam papers, making it easy to match answer to question.

- Where it is necessary to show the answer on a stave, the original stave is printed in grey with the answer shown in black, for example:

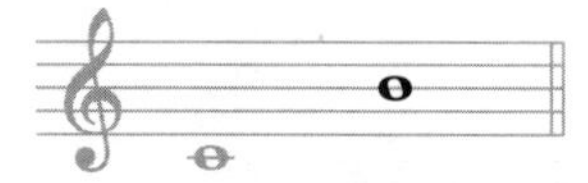

- Alternative answers are separated by an oblique stroke (/) or by *or*, for example:

getting slower / gradually getting slower

- Answers that require the candidate to write out a scale, chord or triad have been shown at one octave only. Reasonable alternatives at different octaves can also receive full marks.

Theory Paper Grade 4 2010 B
Model Answers

1 (a) 60 dotted minims in a minute / 60 dotted half notes in a minute / 60 dotted minim beats in a minute / 60 dotted half-note beats in a minute (2)

graceful / gracefully / with grace (2)

held back / getting slower / gradually getting slower (2)

(b) D / D major (2)

(c) (3)

(d) (4)

Moderato ♩. = 60
dolce e molto grazioso

p *cresc.* **riten.** **a tempo** *f*

2 *There are many ways of completing this question. Either of the specimen completions below would receive full marks.* (10)

EITHER

(a)

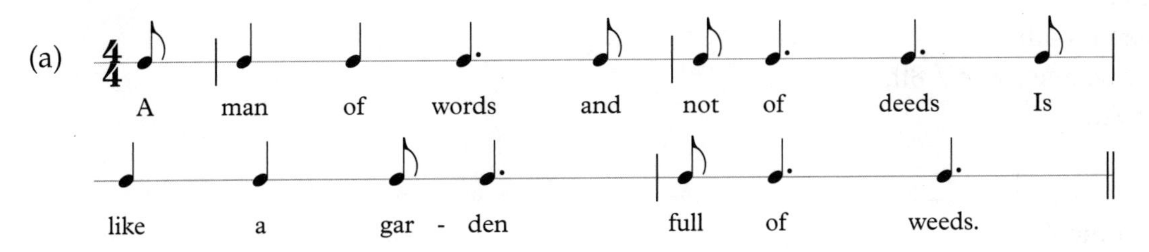

OR

(b)

3 (a) (i) in an undertone / below the voice (2)

accent / forced / accented (2)

getting quieter / gradually getting quieter (2)

(ii) *vif* *animé* (4)

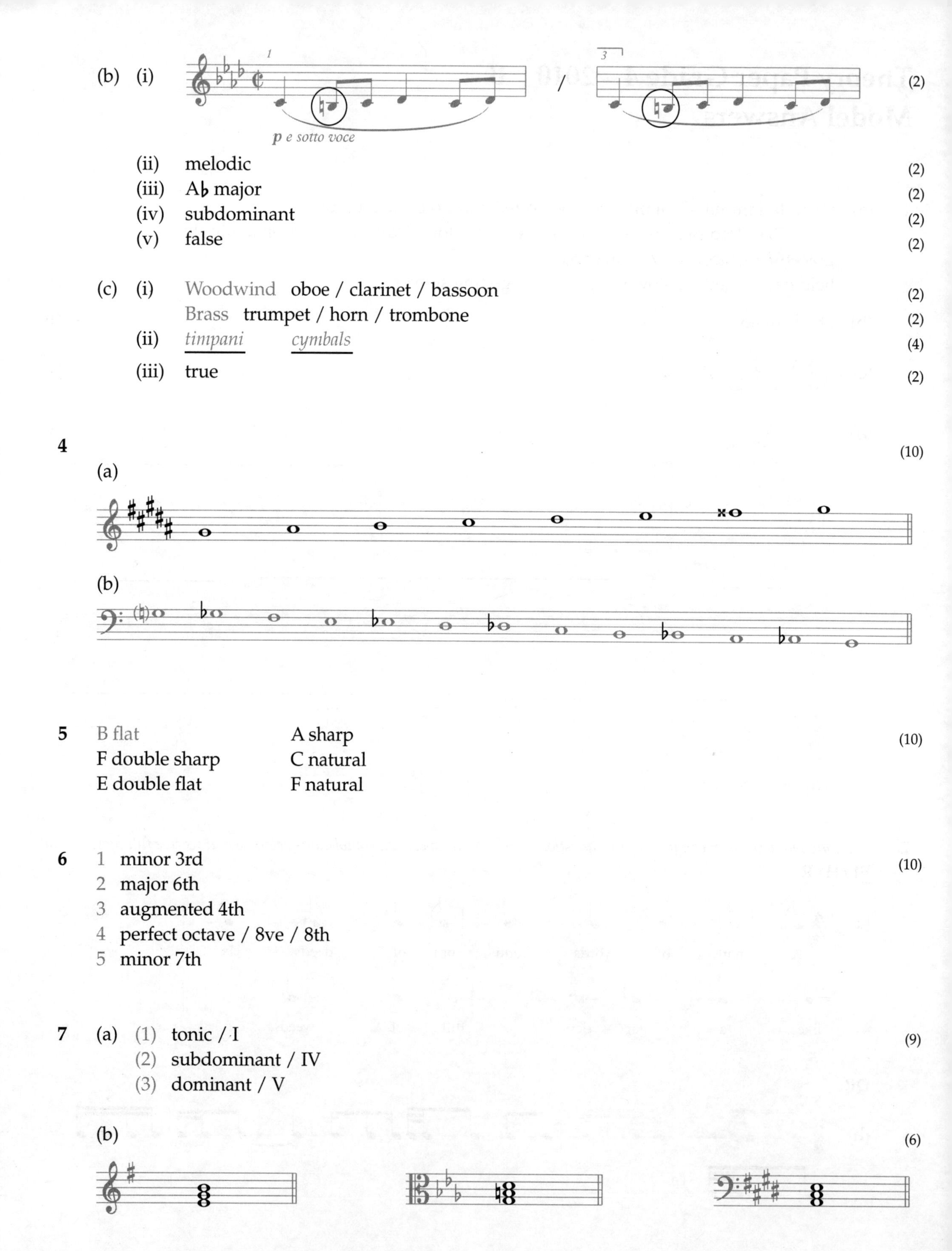

(b) (i) (2)

(ii) melodic (2)

(iii) A♭ major (2)

(iv) subdominant (2)

(v) false (2)

(c) (i) Woodwind oboe / clarinet / bassoon (2)

Brass trumpet / horn / trombone (2)

(ii) *timpani* *cymbals* (4)

(iii) true (2)

4 (10)

(a)

(b)

5 (10)

B flat	A sharp
F double sharp	C natural
E double flat	F natural

6 (10)

1 minor 3rd
2 major 6th
3 augmented 4th
4 perfect octave / 8ve / 8th
5 minor 7th

7 (a) (9)

(1) tonic / I
(2) subdominant / IV
(3) dominant / V

(b) (6)

Theory Paper Grade 4 2010 C
Model Answers

1 (a) slow / stately (2)
majestic (2)
more loud / louder (2)

(b) 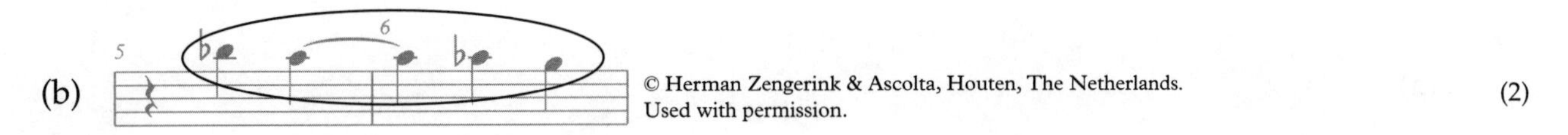
 (2)

(c) lower mordent / inverted mordent / mordent (2)

(d) 9 (2)

(e) 

(2)

(f) 12 (1)

2 *There are many ways of completing this question. Either of the specimen completions below would receive full marks.* (10)

EITHER

(a) 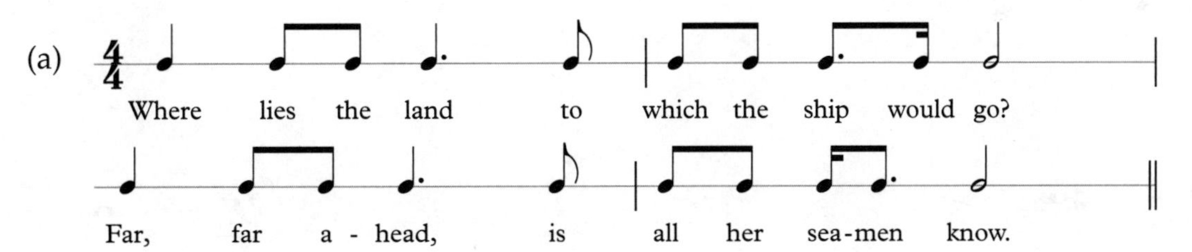

OR

(b) 

3 (a) (i) lively, but not too much / quick, but not too much (4)
with mutes / muted (2)
accent / forced / accented (2)
(ii) *vif* (2)

(b) (i) diminished 5th (2)
(ii) (4)
(iii) E (2)
(iv) F♯ / F sharp (2)

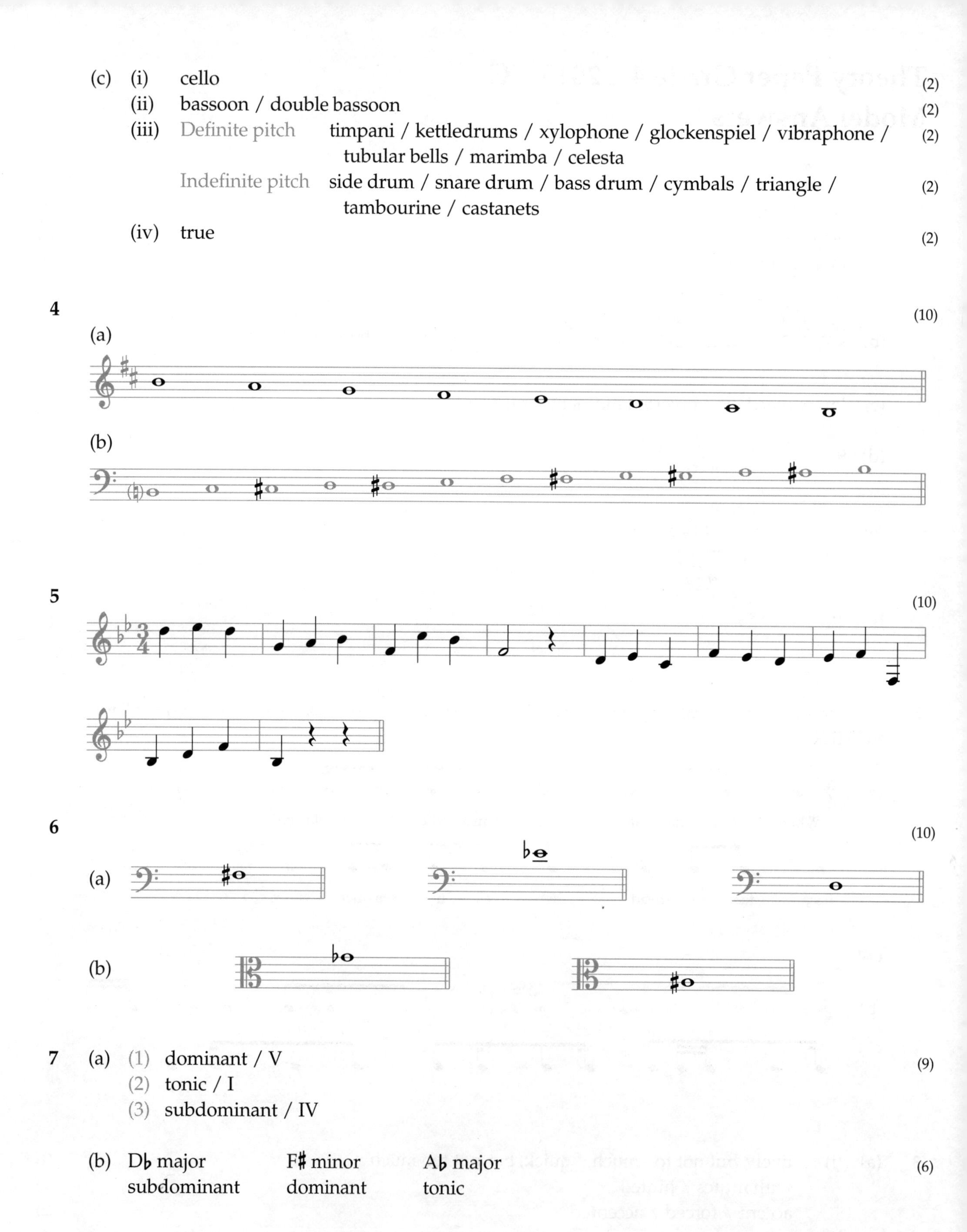

(c) (i) cello (2)

(ii) bassoon / double bassoon (2)

(iii) Definite pitch: timpani / kettledrums / xylophone / glockenspiel / vibraphone / tubular bells / marimba / celesta (2)

Indefinite pitch: side drum / snare drum / bass drum / cymbals / triangle / tambourine / castanets (2)

(iv) true (2)

4 (10)

(a)

(b)

5 (10)

6 (10)

(a)

(b)

7 (a) (1) dominant / V (9)

(2) tonic / I

(3) subdominant / IV

(b) (6)

D♭ major	F♯ minor	A♭ major
subdominant	dominant	tonic

Theory Paper Grade 4 2010 S
Model Answers

1 (a) not too cheerful / not too lively / not too fast / not too quick (3)
play the notes smoothly / slur (1)

(b) compound (2)
quadruple

(c) mordent / upper mordent (2)

(d) (2)

(e) (3)

(f) (2)

2 *There are many ways of completing this question. Either of the specimen completions below would receive full marks.* (10)

EITHER

(a)

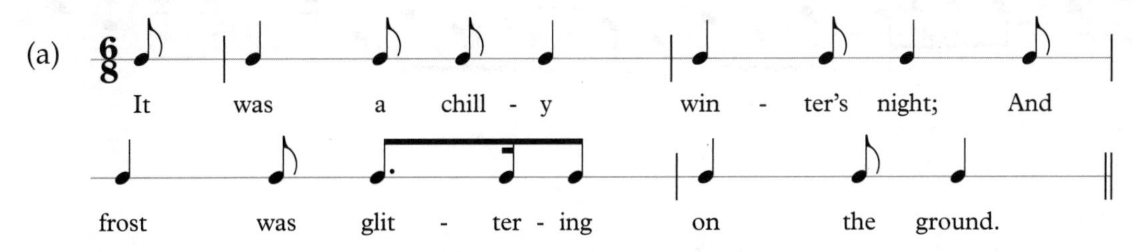

OR

(b)

3 (a) (i) majestic / stately (2)
in a military style / marching (2)
accent / forced / accented (2)

(ii) two / two quavers / two eighth notes / one crotchet / one quarter note / one beat / four semiquavers / four 16th notes (2)

(iii) false (2)

(b) (i) supertonic (2)
(ii) (2)
(iii) perfect 4th (2)
(iv) (2)
(v) 6 (2)
(c) (i) flute / oboe / clarinet (2)
(ii) tuba / bass tuba (2)
(iii) viola (2)
(iv) horn violin (4)
4 (10)
(a)
(b)
5 (10)
6 (10)
(a)
(b)
7 (a) (1) subdominant / IV (9)
(2) tonic / I
(3) dominant / V
(b) (6)

Support material for ABRSM Music Theory exams

Theory of Music Exams
Past Papers
Grades 1 to 8 (separately)

Music Theory in Practice
Grades 1 to 8 (separately)

Music Theory in Practice
Model Answers
Grades 1 to 5 (separately)

The AB Guide to
Music Theory
Parts I and II

First Steps in
Music Theory
Grades 1–5

ABRSM's mission is to motivate musical achievement. We aim to support the development of learners and teachers in music education worldwide and to celebrate their achievements. We do this through authoritative and internationally recognized assessments, publications and professional development support for teachers, and through charitable donations.

ABRSM
24 Portland Place
London W1B 1LU
United Kingdom

www.abrsm.org

Published by ABRSM (Publishing) Ltd,
a wholly owned subsidiary of ABRSM

Printed in England by Halstan & Co. Ltd,
Amersham, Bucks 10/10

ISBN 978-1-84849-297-4